Saving Our Daughters

From A Man's Point of View VOL.1

CURTIS BENJAMIN | KAREN WATTS M.Ed.

Library of Congress Control Number: 2008940628

Front Cover Photo Credits include:
Photo Illustration - Cats Meow Communications; Gary Sturgis - Photo
provided by Inez Lewis Photography; T.I. - Photo provided by Darren
Ankenman; Sean Garrett - Photo provided by Derek Blanks; Deon Grant
- Photo provided by Eric M. Croas | Cats Meow Communications; Anwan
Glover - Photo provided by Roy Cox ; Lamman Rucker - Photo provided by
UMA Worldwide

Inside Photo Credits include:
Anwan Glover (p. 37) - Roy Cox; T.I. (p. 51) - Darren Ankenman; Deon
Grant (p. 65) - Eric M. Croas | Cats Meow Communications; Various
Community Photos in the Intermission section (p. 72-73; 92-93) - It's Cool
To Be Smart & Cat's Meow Communications; Sean Garrett (p. 100) - Ben
Watts; Lamman Rucker (p. 113) - UMA Worldwide; Gary Sturgis (p. 128) -
Inez Lewis Photography

Back Cover Photo Credits include:
Photographer - Alpha Phi Alpha Brother Frederick Anderson; Make Up
Artist - Vanessa Carter; Wardrobe Stylist - Lisa Harris

Legal Services and Clearances provided by:
The Law Office of Omara S. Harris, Esq., LLC
P.O. Box 19199 Atlanta, Georgia 31126

First Printing 2008
Printed in the United States of America
ISBN 978-0-615-27037-1

"But seek ye first the kingdom of GOD, and his righteousness; and all these things shall be added unto you."

- Matthew 6:33

"This scripture was a special request for me to study from my mother, to guide me as a man, husband and as a father."

- Curtis Benjamin

PLAYBILL

SAVING OUR DAUGHTERS
FROM A MAN'S POINT OF VIEW

PLAYBILL

SAVING OUR DAUGHTERS
FROM A MAN'S POINT OF VIEW

OPENING
MONOLOGUE

To the reader;

Many of the ills of our present day society and culture seem insurmountable. It seems that we as people have forgotten some things. One is the importance of children, another being the connection between our thoughts and our reality. It seems that we also have lost sight that it is important for a member of a strongly functioning community to have a sense of purpose.

Children have to be taught the ways of the world. They cannot be left to their own devices for they have none. Someone or something will always be their guide. A child's first years are critical to that child's development. It is only through the guidance of adults that youth will obtain the skill sets they need to be successful and contributing members of their society.

When I started this, my mind regarded this work as a study of today's circumstances. It was a view of what men think, what women need to hear and what women need to absorb. However, as the days and the weeks and the interviews went on, I came to realize that this project that I have been blessed to be a part of is larger than I could have imagined. As my work progressed, it became more than obvious that this was not just about identifying issues, but it was more about healing from those identified wounds.

The scope of this work moved from simple recognition to an inspirational enlightenment. In many respects, it became a God ordained 'how to get through' manual. Through my involvement with this project, I have gained a new Spiritual sister, and a deeper connection with my biological, my Greek and my universal family for which I will be forever grateful. I have learned so much from the gentlemen that I was graciously allowed to interview, and I wish the same for you. Enjoy and be enlightened.

Sincerely,

Karen Watts m.Ed.

PRELUDE TO THE
OPENING ACT

One Woman's Opening Prayer to Men:

I am about to share with you what I face
and live with daily in hopes that you, my
brothers, can prevent anything like this
from ever happening again through your
brotherhood. I am a mother whose daughter, my
most prized possession, was victimized, and it
happened because I wanted to be comfortable
and married.

I have been married most of my adult life,
and with this being my second marriage, I was
determined to make it work regardless of the
cost. Little did I truly realize what "at all
cost" would mean to my daughter's well-being.

My second husband was what you call a
functioning alcoholic. He maintained his job
and appeared to be a good husband, a good
provider and a good family man. I grew up
without much money, but now because of this
man, my daughters and I were provided with a
lot of material comforts. I also was the one
that my family turned to when they needed
someone to bail them out financially. But, my
children (who came from my first marriage)
and I lived a private hell that not many knew of.

My husband would come home drunk, angry and
violent more nights than not, and he would be
verbally abusive to my girls and I. He always
claimed that he did not remember punching
holes in our walls or urinating in our closets.

My husband was not kid-friendly at all. When
he would come home after work and a night
at the bar, my kids and I would retreat to
the safety of our bedrooms allowing him to
unwind downstairs in front of the television.
So on the night he said, "Oh Nikki can stay

down here and watch TV with me," I actually thought he was trying to change.

Nikki is the older of my two daughters and she was always a direct target of my husband's abuse. According to him, she could not do anything right. So I was happy when he seemed to be taking an interest in her. I had not been feeling well that day, and my husband knew it. He told me to go upstairs and take a nap. "We'll be okay," he said convincingly.

I was tired so I went ahead. An hour or so later I woke up and went to look in Nikki's room, but she wasn't there. From the top of the stairs, I called her name three or four times before my husband answered with a story about how they could not hear because the TV was up loud. He told me to just go back to sleep, and again I just obeyed him without question.

I woke up again around 11 p.m. and again went looking in Nikki's room. She still wasn't there, and this time I walked downstairs to where they were. As they heard me coming, I heard my daughter jump up and run into the downstairs bathroom and slam the door behind her.

I walked over and knocked with concern. Nikki slowly opened the door and looked at me the same way a deer looks when startled by a set of headlights. I asked what was wrong because I had heard her throwing up. Before Nikki could answer, my husband came up behind me, "She'll be okay," he said. "She just needs to come and sit back down with me."

"No, she's coming upstairs with me now," I told him. "It's late, she obviously isn't feeling well, and she has to go to school tomorrow."

My husband seemed angry, but he did not try to stop us. I took Nikki to her room and went back to mine. About 10 minutes later, I decided to go back to check on her. To my surprise, he was sitting next to her on the bed and stroking her hair.

I again foolishly thought he was just taking a fatherly interest in her. Now I wonder if I was just that blind, or whether I didn't want to see what was staring me in the face.

A few weeks later, I left the house after one of our many arguments. The girls and I went to a hotel, and I guess Nikki finally felt safe enough to tell me what happened. As the words came spilling out, I just looked at her in shock and disbelief.

She shared that the night I came downstairs, her stepfather was sexually molesting her. He had performed oral sex on her and had forced her to do the same to him. She had run into the bathroom to purge the aftertaste and shame of his penis being in her mouth. She also told me that when I saw him in her room later, he was telling her not to say anything.

I immediately drove back to my home and kicked him out. He claimed not to remember doing anything to Nikki and begged me not to destroy our family. I am least proud of what happened over the next few months.

I did not press charges against my husband because my daughter begged me not to. I admit that I agreed with her because I just wanted this to go away. My girls urged me to let him come home, because they did not want to lose their material comforts. I found that absurd. So I called family members that I trust, but they were the same family members I had 'sponsored.'

They urged me to let him back, and against my better judgment I let him. To protect her, I sent Nikki away to a boarding school, and I began counseling with my husband. At his persistence, I finally agreed to start a family with him. The in vitro process never took which I thank God for.

Last year I finally left him for good. I told Nikki who cried for a week because she was so happy. We don't talk much about what occurred. Right now, I just pray that the damage I unwittingly allowed to happen has not permanently damaged our relationship. I wish I had been stronger earlier, and I continue to pray that one day I become her mommy and she can just be my little girl.

My brothers, I beg that you realize how every aspect of what you do affects a woman's life in different ways. It does not matter whether if the action is intentional or not. I ask that you always put forward your best and encourage your brothers to do the same. Remember that the Lord and the world are watching.

Sincerely,

A Mother Hoping To Heal

A Daughter's Response to her Mother's
Opening Prayer:

I read the letter to men and thought long
and hard before responding to it. I know
that responding is the best thing for me,
and the best thing for my mother. We have
both been in a holding pattern in our
lives since then, and now it's time for us
to taxi away from the gate so that we can
fly.

First, I need my mother to know that I
forgive her. I forgave her a long time
ago. Couldn't she hear the forgiveness
in my voice when I first told her what
he had done to me? Couldn't she see the
forgiveness in my actions? I stayed with
her, I talked to her and I loved her as I
do now.

I do need her to do something for me
though. I need her to say, "This is what
happened. I apologize for my part in it,
and I forgive myself and am willing to
move on."

I also need her to forgive me. I did not
cause his violence towards me in any way.
That's not what I am asking forgiveness
for, but I wish I had trusted her enough
to scream out for help when he was hurting
me.

I wish I had told her right after
it happened, or in any of the many
opportunities I had before I told her. I
wish I had not felt that I was being 'the
brave one' by keeping it all inside to
protect her.

It is a mother's responsibility to protect her young, not the other way around. So I need for her to say to me, "I forgive you," so that I can say, "This is what happened, and I apologize for my part in it. I forgive myself, and I am willing to move on."

I say to parents, please look out for your daughters and your sisters. Many times we may seem strong and unbreakable, but God created us to all work together. God gave us all a job and your biggest one is to take care of us. Please don't let God or us down, and by you doing 'your job' this won't happen anymore.

Sincerely,

A Loving Daughter

A Professional's Healing Words
Dr. Carman Suzanne Clark

To my sisters who are healing;

It is very difficult for us to navigate our way through this life with limited directions. We do the best we can with the resources and knowledge we have available at the time decisions must be made. Sometimes, what is available to us is not enough. A lot of situations we find ourselves having to deal with are often frustrating, overwhelming, spiritually draining, emotionally crippling, and psychologically painful.

I am an African-American woman with a daughter of my own. And like so many of you, my sisters, I have lived through some ominous moments. I have wondered how God could leave me vulnerable to resident evil. And at times my soul felt weighed down by despair so heavy that it hurt to breathe. Sometimes relief seemed so long in coming that I knew since God was not deaf, He must be ignoring me.

The truth is I was getting in my own way; trying to "fix" things my way and making bad situations worse in the process. I prayed for guidance, but what God provided instead was a voice of reason. Alone and in the quiet moments of my own thoughts, I found peace; the kind of peace that surpasses all understanding. When I finally got to a point of complete surrender, I understood the power of that virtue.

Peace is what the soul seeks in times of trouble and pain. Peace is not only anesthesia for a hurting soul; peace is the healer of a wounded life. Peace brings us to the crossroad of awareness and allows us to see our options. This virtue creates in us the vision of a new beginning. While under the influence of Peace, we can see all things clearly even as chaos reigns. Christ calmed an angry sea by saying simply, "peace, be still." And we must follow his lead.

During those times of raging chaos, call peace into existence. When you are alone with your thoughts, learn to be still. Stop struggling with worry and control what you worry about; stop fighting with the "what ifs" and manage the "what is;" stop being indifferent and choose to do something different instead. The objective is to heal without feeling hindered.

Here are a few areas that sisters and daughters often struggle with and some alternatives to dealing with them.

On having low self-esteem

Do you know what self-esteem is? Self-esteem is the comfort zone of how you feel about what you know about yourself. I ask you, "How do you feel about what you know about yourself?" Can you look the person in the mirror in the eyes and say, "I like what I see; I feel good about me." If you cannot do this when you and God are the only ones watching, then your self-esteem is suffering.

It is time to search your soul; not for fault but for freedom. Most people live life from what I prefer to call, the bottom up. Basically, it goes like this: things happen in life; it affects us emotionally which we experience as physical discomfort. Then the mind takes over and we start to add logic to the fabric of the experience and based on our own unique personality, we start to adopt a paradigm of the meaning of life. Most of our personal paradigms or way of seeing ourselves relative to the rest of the world is not always pleasant. We are too busy caring about the negatives of what other people think.

Now let's reverse the sequence. Look at yourself the way God sees you, from the top down. The spirit of God provides the guidance which your personality receives which in turn influences how you feel about yourself. When viewed from this angle, no matter what comes at you in life, you can rest, assured that the paradigm you live by is not defined by what people think, but what you already know in your own soul.

The secret to maintaining a healthy self-esteem is to see ourselves the way God sees us. Not to exploit the mercy of God to justify sin, but to share testimony of having been saved from it. A wonderful and powerful poem entitled INVICTUS, written by William Ernest Henley (1849-1903) from a hospital bed, after having a foot amputated, (written over 100 years ago) sums up the inherent power of a healthy self-esteem. The point being, when you follow the voice of spiritual reason, there is nothing and no one powerful enough to claim your self-worth.

Invictus

Out of the night that covers me

Black as the pit from pole to pole,

I thank whatever gods may be

For my unconquerable soul

In the fell clutches of circumstance

I have not winced nor cried aloud.

Under the bludgeoning of chance

My head is bloody, but unbowed.

Beyond this place of wrath of tears

Looms but the Horror of the shade,

And yet the menace of the years

Finds, and shall find, me unafraid.

It matters not how strait the gate,

How charged with punishment the scroll,

I am the master of my fate;

I am the captain of my soul.

Enough said.

On struggling with painful life experiences

If you have ever sang in a black church choir, I know most of you will remember the lyrics of this song written by Curtis Burrell and beautifully sung by the late Reverend James Cleveland:

I DON'T FEEL NO WAYS TIRED;

I COME TOO FAR FROM WHERE I STARTED FROM.

NOBODY TOLD ME THAT THE ROAD WOULD BE EASY;

I DON'T BELIEVE HE BROUGHT ME THIS FAR TO LEAVE ME.

In my opinion, this is one of the most powerful Negro hymnals ever penned to paper. Our people's history is rooted in painful life experiences, from our arrival and to this day. As a people, we struggle with collective pain and as individuals we suffer with personal pain. It seems painful life experiences confronts us on all sides. There will always be some form of trouble to deal with and that trouble almost always equals a painful experience, whether it's racism, being victims of crime, injustice, etc.

I am not trying to make these experiences sound simplistic in our ability to overcome them because all of them are felt on a very personal level. What I am saying is that NO ONE has enough authority in this world to tell you what you can or cannot overcome. You are the only one with the power to choose and make that determination for yourself. Because remember. What happens to a person is not as powerful as what happens inside of a person.

The reason I love the lyrics of this song is because it defines who we are as a people and what we already know of ourselves as individual persons. The first line literally gets in front of the struggle and dares the soul to be moved. The second line is confirmation to the latent power of the soul as a sojourner in this wayfaring land. The third line highlights our understanding that God sends rain on the just and the unjust; however, the last line mandates providence.

It states that I am not here by accident. I have a purpose in this life and no matter how difficult the journey becomes; no matter how much negative impact those painful experiences may try to impose on my journey back home; even if it means, "I gotta walk through hell to get to heaven," my struggle, my living and my suffering will not be in vain.

On dealing with medical issues

Healing from medical issues is not always easy. When most people think about medical issues, they automatically think physical discomfort. We sometimes forget that there is a psychological and emotional component to dealing with the medical issues also. To my sisters who are in the midst of healing from a medical issue whether it is cancer, HIV or a flu virus, the key to successful healing is to understand the nature of what ails you.

Learn everything you can about your diagnosis. Know everything you can about the medication(s) prescribed to combat and control the symptoms of the illness. Talk to your treating physician candidly about the facts of your diagnosis and do not settle for being treated with indifference. When it comes to your health, "you need to ask somebody..."

The reason I strongly encourage you to talk about your illness, condition and treatment is because not knowing will keep you feeling bad. Feeling bad often leads to stress and sometimes stressing over a medical situation will kill you faster than the disease itself. Mental worry puts the body at a disadvantage when it is trying to heal. You are not violating any rules of professionalism by questioning your physician about everything concerning your condition. However, here is the most important part. You must be willing to accept the truth and be at peace with the facts surrounding your medical issues. And you must be willing to make the necessary psychological, behavioral, and sometimes life-changing adjustments in your quest for physical healing

On struggling through chemical dependency

Chemical dependency is a demon that no one who really knows the facts wants to take on. Even with faith that can move mountains, you do not want to tempt this wanton fate. Everybody who struggles with chemical dependency started out experimenting with recreational drugs or taking some form of medication to alleviate a physical ailment.

No one woke up one day and decided to become a drug abuser, an addict or chemically dependent, but if you find yourself in any of these chemically dependent categories, it is time to stop kidding yourself and assess the quality of your life. Ask yourself, "Do you want to live out the rest of your life being held hostage to the physical vices of a chemical?" "Do you like having your soul chained to the physical effects of a drug?" "Do you really believe that abusing a drug can help you heal?"

Chemical dependency will always bring you to a crossroad of choice because eventually the habitual abuse of any drug will start to demand that you make sacrifices, either in favor of your life or in favor of the drug. Chronic drug use and experimenting with so-called recreational drugs often lead to chemical dependency and it is an endless road to nowhere.

Once your life becomes hostage to the devices of the chemical dependent demon, you will be running away from them for the rest of your life, or it will lay claim to your life and everyone in it. The various reasons why some people struggle with chemical dependency are personal in nature, and there is no cure that is "one size fits all." However, in order to heal from its devastating effects you must be willing to make a conscious decision to stop poisoning your body unnecessarily. It's your choice.

On losing a loved one

For most people, death is rarely even thought of. The finality of this transition is too uncomfortable to worry about. We would prefer to go about our daily lives treating death as something that visits other people. But it is this very revulsion to death that makes our painful reactions to its reality so difficult to accept.

I'm not saying we have to walk around talking about death and dying as a part of normal conversation. What I am saying is we have to stop being afraid to die.

This has two very important and immediate effects on the soul. First, the soul that is not afraid to die is not afraid to live, and second, a living soul never dies. We are creations of God. We are the only ones of God's creations that He literally breathed life into and when He did this, "Man became a living soul."

The death of the body is inevitable and unavoidable. It is a bitter reality of this life but it is not the end of life. My hope is that you establish an honest relationship with God before your time occurs. Because the soul who is at peace with their own crossing, will be at peace with the crossing of others, including loved ones. It is okay to mourn, grieve, and remember, but it is not okay to cling.

Remember that in your memories, lives the soul of the one you grieve for. You are on this healing journey together. My prayer for you is that someday you can smile instead of cry when you think of each other, and eventually both you and the one for whom you grieve will be healed enough to move on and be at peace.

On surviving sexual abuse, incest, and rape

Devastating shock, immobilizing fear, catatonic state, angry, frightened, frustrated, powerless, impaired, paralyzed; pick a word, any word. All of them fit.

The damages wrought on the mind, body and soul of a victim of any sexual crime are incalculable. It is hard to imagine a more disgusting crime than the sexual violation of one person committed against another. No one, no age, no gender has escaped the maniacal ravages of a sexual predator, and the devastation they leave behind in their attempts to dismiss themselves from their victim's pain cannot be put into words.

There is no such thing as a "nice" child molester or a "kind" rapist. These people are cold, calculating, predators who prey on innocence and vulnerability. They are monsters who prove the existence of evil by the very nature of why they do what they do. Sexual assault of any kind is about stealing and gaining power, and it is ALWAYS a premeditated act.

These cowards prey on someone whom they think cannot or will not fight back. This is only the beginning of what you deal with when you cross paths with a sexual predator, but I don't want to waste time talking about them. My support is overwhelmingly for the victim, the silent sufferers, you my sisters, who have survived this crime.

First of all, let me say this. What happened to you is not and was not your fault. Let me say that again. *What happened to you is not and was not your fault.* You have no control over the behavior of another adult.

Silent sufferers tend to beat themselves up with illogical ramblings; trying to negotiate with incomprehensible and impossible self-guilt, and berate themselves with mind-numbing questions such as, "maybe I could have stopped it if I had been more careful," "I should have seen this coming;" or some other form of trying to convince yourself that there must have been something you could have done to stop this from happening.

Silent sufferers also tend to self-isolate, hiding in dark psychological corners i.e. shame, embarrassment, and depression. Life hurts… and the pain is compounded by unsuccessful attempts to mend the enormous hole that has formed in the center of a broken heart which in turn, leaves the soul feeling empty and beyond repair.

My sisters, I understand; not as a therapist, but as a sister in arms. I have been there. I know full well that the most difficult part of healing from this kind of pain is belief that healing can actually take place. It is so easy to get stuck on that endless rhetorical question of "why me?"

Would you prefer it happened to someone else? I have to believe the answer is no. If we are to move forward from this standpoint, then we must be willing to come out on the other side of this pain and redefine what it means to feel whole. You who have survived this evil, did so because of something God gave you your spirit, His spirit, the one He breathed into us at the beginning of creation.

At the core of our existence, when life feels like a waste of time, something inside of you responds to the power of prayer and will not allow you to give up. This soul's power is stronger than anything that exists in this world because it reminds you that no matter how bad life feels, you have a right to exist. You have a right to fight back with a resource a predator will never be able to comprehend or conquer. Refuse to stay broken. Remember the words of Paul from 2 Corinthians 4:6-10, because they apply so beautifully to the latent power of God's spirit that resides in us all and will take up the fight for us when we can't.

Paul wrote "For it is God who commanded light to shine out of darkness, who has shown in our hearts, to give the light of the knowledge of the glory of God in the face of Jesus Christ; but we have this treasure in earthen vessels, that the excellence of this power may be of God and not of us; (even though) we are afflicted in every way; (we are) not crushed; perplexed, but not despairing; persecuted but not forsaken; struck down, but not destroyed."

It was the very essence of God's light; the same power that moved Christ beyond the pain of His broken body to fulfill His purpose on the cross, this same power moves us when we refuse to stay broken. You cannot allow this offense to define you or your life. Oprah Winfrey and Maya Angelou, sisters-in-arms, are two examples of how powerful in spirit you can evolve into when you refuse to stay broken and allow yourself to heal. I had to create passion out of my own pain. Because I realized while on that journey toward healing, that if I did not learn to love myself, help myself, and nurture the spirit of myself, or that if I did not reach back deep enough into my past to help my sisters and their daughters find their future, then I would have failed in my purpose and God (literally) saved my life for nothing.

If you want to heal, focus on what you want to create, not just on what you want to change. Reach out to someone in the same pain; helping someone heal from their pain has a miraculous self-healing affect all of its own. Talk to someone who understands, and last but certainly not least, believe in the healing power of prayer rest assured that when you've done all that you can, just stand.

To my brothers

Your sisters who are healing from this kind of pain need to

know that decent brothers "got their back." We need to hear from you, and we need to hear of you getting in the face of any brother who would disrespect and/or violate any of our sisters so horribly.

The list of actual victims is far too long. We need your help to stop this evil. You are the masculine image of respect and strength we need to see more of and hear more from. Seeing you speak out on our behalf makes sisters feel all the more confident that you care.

When a female is violated in such a way, she has a tendency to generalize her pain. Not deliberately; but figuratively. Don't let these monsters speak for you. It is important for sisters, i.e. mothers, daughters, nieces, cousins, aunts, friends, etc. to see you speaking against this evil so she'll have somewhere to place her future hopes for a healthy relationship, especially for our daughters.

Dr. Carman Suzanne Clark

Copyright ©2003

For more about Dr. Clark and contact information see page 148

"After reading the PRELUDE TO THE OPENING ACT involving the dialog between the mother and daughter, it's clear that we all need to celebrate the fact they were strong enough to actually communicate their true feelings to one another and loved each other without condition enough for their relationship to survive.

Many might say that the topic and text of domestic violence and sexual abuse should only be targeted to adults. However, life's realities prove that everyone should be informed about what happens to 1 of 3 women in our neighborhoods, communities and families. More importantly, everyone should be challenged to make a difference."

-E. Walter Smith - Singer/Songwriter/The Tenderness Campaign

ACT I

"Approximately 43% of teen dating violence victims reported that the dating abuse they experienced occurred in a school building or on school grounds."

~ Christian Molidor and Richard M. Tolman, "Gender and contextual factors in adolescent dating violence," Violence Against Women, Vol 4, no. 2 (1998)

To Whom It May Concern:

The funeral was today, and I still cannot believe she is gone. As I stand in the middle of her room, I can still hear the laughter and giggles shared with friends as they talk about boys, clothes, comments posted on their MySpace pages, or the latest video they saw on YouTube. I look at the pictures of cheerleading camp and her sophomore Homecoming Dance.

The young man in that particular photo brings back the memory of when she brought him home to meet the family. As a father, I never expected any boy to be good enough for her, but this young football star caught me off-guard. He was respectful, had good grades and a plan in place for a higher education and the ability to support a family of his own some day.

How could I have known that he had begun to emotionally abuse my daughter, or that he had the nerve to put his hands on her? Was there a way I could have saved her before things escalated the way they did?

People have told me that violence is just another thing that teens have to navigate in school. I always thought it was reserved for the gangbangers and the kids who felt outcast. I never imagined it would be my daughter that would find herself on the receiving end of a cold steel hunting knife. That it was done by the same respectful adolescent with a hidden dark side rips my own heart out.

I cannot figure out why my daughter did

not tell us what he was doing to her. Was she afraid how we would react? Did she feel that it was her own fault? Even worse, could it be that she tried to tell us, but we did not hear exactly what she was saying?

It is tragic that I will never know the exact answer to that question. It is even more horrible to know that I will never hear her laughter, see her smile, or feel her hug ever again. All I can do is embrace the memories and pray for peace. I also hope that others will hear of my loss and be able to rescue their own daughters if needed.

Sincerely,

A Broken-Hearted Father

"Don't settle for less."

~ Anwan Glover

Fans of the HBO series The Wire will know and recognize Anwan Glover (a.k.a. Big G) as Slim Charles. His entertainment resume also includes appearances on Law & Order, the films Hood Related and Divided City, the Go-Go band Backyard Band (a.k.a. BYB), and music video appearances including Vivian Green's Gotta Go Gotta Leave, Rick Ross The Biggest Boss, Lil Mo's Boys wit Cash, and Raheem Devaughn's Guess Who Loves You More among others. He also has done modeling and co-owns a clothing line Bodego Sport and production company Bodego Film Productions.

As a native of Washington D.C., Anwan is no stranger to the violence of the streets. He was only 9 when he committed his first crime. At 13, he was the victim of the hot lead from a fired gun. Unfortunately, it would not be the last bullet to enter his body as he has been shot on eight other separate occasions. It was this upbringing that guided him to give back to that same community by working to decrease the violence through various venues including It's Cool To Be Smart. "When I speak to kids in the program, I tell them to look at me and how my life has unfolded," said Anwan. "I don't spare the sordid details about how I grew up; because I want them to know that you can break the cycle and change for better."

His passion for inspiring our daughters and community youth was evident during our conversation for the book. In fact, he was clear when discussing the mistakes of his own youth and how the loss of his own brother has affected him.

I made mistakes in the past. I had an older brother that was in the street. It was just like when you wake up in the morning and you see your older brother putting his clothes on, strapping his gun to his waist, getting his drugs and leaving to go take care of his business. And you see that every day in the vicinity of where you live and you come home from school and you see that.

You don't have to be a part of that, but eventually kids fall into that trap. I was fortunate to get out of it you know what I mean. I've made mistakes in my past. I made wrong decisions in different situations; including getting into that gang violence with my older brother. We just got embedded in things we didn't really want to be in, and my little brother use to look up to me. I used to tell him, 'I'm going to make it. I'm going to make it for us,' and he used to be like, 'Man, you're my hero.'

My little brother was always fascinated by seeing me on stage, and just seeing me out in a crowd performing. Yeah, he would really be proud because right before my brother was killed, I was filming the last episode of *The Wire*. He was just so excited. He had gotten older, and you know as you get older you just don't show as much emotion. But he would be so excited. He would be so proud of me because of what I'm doing, and how I'm giving back to the community with the kids. Just trying to preach that thing every day with the non-violence and knowing what's going on in our community.

As we talked a bit more about his work on *The Wire*, he shared that one of the things he has personally taken from his experience is that life is about family and growth because of the family-oriented feel on the set. I asked how young ladies can draw the same conclusion about family and growth in the real world.

I can turn that into a lot with the young ladies. I talk

to young sisters a lot, and, I just have different ways of coming at young sisters. I ask them different things. Like a couple of weeks ago I shared this with somebody.

These three young ladies were like 'Ahh, that's the guy from *The Wire*, and I was like 'Hey, what's up?'

They wanted to take pictures and I was like 'Hey how y'all doing in school?' they said, 'Ahh, we doing okay.' Then I said, 'How many of y'all got boyfriends?' 'We do, we got boyfriends,' and I asked, 'how many of you are practicing safe sex?' Two of them raised their hands.

I told them that's a real big part of your life. I mean first of all there are diseases and once you bring a child into this world, you have it for life, and you're not financially stable. You have a lot on your mind. You can't let these little young guys talk you into doing something you don't want to do. It's always a life change. Like you're a young sister and your mother had to bring you into this world.

Then I asked them how many of them had their dads at home. One of them got kind of upset with me because I guess she has some issues at home. So I tried to address them and express that family thing over to them like from the show.

I just tried to talk to the little sisters and let them know it's all about family first and taking your time and making good choices in life. Everybody's doing this and doing that, and a lot of girls are sexually active but you've got to make the right steps. I'm not saying not to do it, but 9 times out of 10 we have to keep them from making the wrong mistakes.

So I turn it all different kinds of ways, and I get a lot of their attention. I keep it real because when you sugarcoat it, they may not get it. It just depends on what environment I'm in and who I am speaking to. I go in on their level then break it down. I go in trying to make them comfortable first, and talk to them about different things to get their attention.

As our conversation became more comfortable, we brought up the sensitive subject of foreigners basing their opinions of African-American women based on lyrics and film images. We asked him what his view of black women would be if he were from another country and bombarded with these images.

Umm, if I was from another country, what would I think of black women? I watch a lot of TV and I watch foreign countries' television shows. A lot of people do look at our women as degraded sometimes. They look at us like all we have is the hoochie look just bouncing around in videos, but there are a lot of intelligent black women in high places. They just don't portray those. They just don't show those sides of our women.

If I was from another country, I would not know that side either. I think this could be changed if we have had more shows showing what our black sisters are really doing. What they are doing for the country, because we have a lot of strong black women who are out here doing a lot.

Those other countries need to read the good magazines like *Essence* and *Ebony*. There are so many different outlets that we should push forward. You know in Atlanta the CDC has the 'Wrap It Up' campaign. You know if they see it more it will be practiced more.

With this whole situation I think it's the same way.

Have shows showing black women doing more and better things than just bouncing around in videos. They should be portrayed differently.

Talking about the CDC "Wrap It Up" campaign reminded us of a young girl we recently heard on talk radio saying "Nowadays we don't really worry about that, we just worry about our clothes and our music, our cars and stuff like that." While we certainly had our own opinion, we asked for Anwan's take on it.

Ugh. A lot of them are worried more about getting the newest purse or outfit instead of worrying about getting an HIV test. It's tough. I talk to them and let them know. I might cut out a picture. I get a video vixen's picture, I get a working class woman's picture, and I get a picture of a young woman with four or five kids, and I compare them. We are chasing the wrong things.

I ask them, 'Out of the pictures, who do you think is more likely to get HIV?' None of them knows, but there are statistics that show it would likely be the one with the video vixen's body, driving a BMW and carrying a Gucci bag. If you're not using condoms you're just crazy.

As our conversation took on a more relaxed tone, we discovered the women in Anwan's life are his personal role models.

My sister is inspiring, because she had my niece at a young age. No matter what she went through she managed to always keep a job, and she didn't wait for assistance from the government. She continued working all the way through nine whole months of pregnancy.

I thought that was really strong, (especially) to be a

strong black woman to be in her condition. To continue working and she made sure she had saved her money for her daughter so that she would be able to have a life, you know what I mean.

Like my sister, there is also my aunt and my mom. My mom took care of us. She worked two or three jobs no matter what. There was never a father figure around. Those three women, I was raised by them and I looked up to them. I was raised by women, and I turned out pretty good (laughter).

They would be inspiring to girls now because if they watched the ways my mom, my sister and my aunt did things back then, they would see that they did so many things. Nowadays there are so many ways to get assistance. Girls today have so many lazy ways.

There was welfare back then too, but to see them work, to leave one job, come home and fix dinner on Friday to have some fish in the pan and some cornbread. Then they would leave out to go to their evening job, and when they get off their evening job to go right back to the first job and still try to do a part-time job. I saw that hustle, and that's what my young sisters today need to see to succeed and make it in life.

Hearing the influence his sister, mom and aunt have had, we wondered what qualities Anwan would be looking for in a young lady if he were looking for a potential girlfriend or spouse.

I would want her to know what she wants to be or where she would like to be in five years. I would want her to be a genuine person. She doesn't really have to worry about a material life. She just needs to worry about where she wants her family to be eventually and just what she wants to do. You want to have a genuine person in your corner. Also, she has to have a genuine life. She doesn't have to do what I do. She just has to have goals for herself and her family.

As we finished the conversation, Anwan provided some final advice for his young black sisters.

The largest piece of advice I would give young ladies is to treat yourself like you want to be treated. Reach for the stars. Focus and have something in life. Try to reach some real high goals.

If no one in your family has graduated from school, you be the first one. Set yourself to the next level. The smallest piece of advice I would give would be to never let anyone put you down. You got to look at yourself in the mirror.

I think I pretty much covered it (laughter). Just be positive.

To my young sisters just realize that you are our backbone; our strength. Without you there would be no future. Never disrespect yourself and never let yourself be disrespected.

REFLECTION PERIOD

REFLECTION PERIOD

"I once contemplated suicide and woulda tried, but when I held that 9, all I could see was my momma's eyes..."

~ Tupac Shakur – Thugz Mansion (Better Dayz) November 2002

To Whom It May Concern:

LaTonya and my daughter have been friends for years. They even decided to go to the same college and be roommates. I have always considered LaTonya a part of our family, and she has been like another daughter to me.

I have felt kind of responsible for her, since she has not had a father around and all, but lately I haven't liked the path LaTonya has been on. She stopped listening to me, and I have stopped trying. I warned my daughter not to be dragged down too. You see, my daughter and LaTonya started clubbing one night a week, then two nights a week, then four, and so on. I sat my girl down and told her this kind of behavior would not be accepted. There was no way she could concentrate on her classes and be hanging out so much. She had to make a choice, and since I'm paying her bills, she better listen to me or make other arrangements to cover her expenses. Unlike LaTonya, my daughter listened and heard what I was saying.

Soon after that talk, my daughter thanked me because LaTonya was acting crazy, and she was so happy that she had listened to me. My daughter shared that LaTonya met some guy at the club and was losing out on everything. She said that the guy had her doing all kinds of things, including dancing at a strip club and giving him the money she made.

LaTonya's grades had become so bad that she was facing academic probation or worse.

My daughter also shared that the boy had other girlfriends besides LaTonya. I told my daughter that all we could do was pray for her.

I knew that things were bad for LaTonya, but I was not prepared for the news I would receive. That day my daughter ran to me crying hysterically after the police had just left her house. Apparently they discovered the dead bodies of LaTonya and her boyfriend. They were found in a car with something stuck in the exhaust pipe.

Inside of her purse, they found a note LaTonya had written stating that her boyfriend told her he had AIDS and was going to die. It also said that he planned to take his own life before it got too bad. She wrote that he loved her and wanted them to be together in the next life. LaTonya stated that she had never had a love like this and wanted to die with him. In the fateful note, she asked me to tell her mama that she loved her.

I thank you God for saving my daughter.

Sincerely,

A Relieved Father

"Women are the origin of life. Women are the backbone of the world."

~ T.I.

T.I. (known in Hollywood as Clifford Harris) has grown to truly become one of his generation's most captivating speakers. Be it a frank conversation with a roomful of youth about the positive side of staying in school and following their dreams or moving thousands of fans during a concert; audiences are engrossed by the King of the South's words.

So it is no surprise that T.I. had a hypnotic effect on a group of mothers and daughters at the first annual "It's Cool To Be Smart Saving Our Daughters Speaking Panel," along with his fellow celebrity fathers. After the panel, I looked forward to further discussing societies misperception of black fathers in our community.

He is well known as Mr. Harris, and of course everybody recognizes the entertainment persona T.I. or TIP. Given his status as an entertainer, I wondered how he integrates being a celebrity with fatherhood, and how he felt Hip Hop has affected men's relationships with women?

I don't integrate the two. My celebrity provides the finances for my family. Being a celebrity allows me to provide the best for my family, but being a celebrity is not a part of my family.

Positive injections in our society have to start off small. In order for anything to work it has to have a "cool factor" for today's generation. Someone with the "cool factor" is someone that the kids will listen to. Kayne West has it and has made going to college cool. Kayne is proud of the fact that he has gone to college. I do not know anything about him finishing but he went.

Common has it with being an example of a positive black man. The same is true of Lupe Fiasco as well. Lupe Fiasco burst on the scene in 2006. He won a Grammy in 2008 and was also nominated for a whole host of awards in 2007.

I'd also like to think that I have it. I've walked on both sides in my life. I've done some not so good things in my past, and I'm trying to do good things in my future. The sky's the limit. I think there will be a new breed of superstars. Hip-Hop will expand into new genres. I'm excited about Hip-Hop's future.

The conversation quickly moved to the business side of Hip-Hop and how it makes money. The intensity level of the conversation rose as we discussed how society views the Hip-Hop culture with women in a negative way.

Americas buying power rests on sexism and violence. There was sexism and violence in America way before there was a T.I. or Hip-Hop, and there will be that sexism and violence way after.

Like I said it's about supply and demand. Why do you think porn is a billion dollar industry? America is built on supply and demand. It doesn't matter how negative the images are in Hip-Hop, if our society continues wanting it then Hip-Hop will keep providing it. Hip-Hop is the elephant in the room. It is the youngest and the newest genre. It is influential and threatening to middle-America, especially because of who some of the consumers of rap music are. Not to mention that rap is dominated by young African-American males. Hip-Hop provides a threat and it intimidates. We have a voice to the masses, and if we organize we could influence anything.

Upbringing includes your family and your environment. Society has to change its desires for things to change.

After speaking about Hip-Hop, the conversation transitioned into discussing family. I congratulated him on his new family situation, and asked what he tells his sons to look for in a woman.

I also asked how he would respond if his daughter came home with a black eye or a bruise and some story about how she fell or how she ran into something, but it was obvious that her boyfriend caused her injury.

I tell them to follow their hearts. I tell them to be with someone who has their best interest in mind. You want to be with someone who wants you not just what you have.

Whew, that second one is tough. I'd like to say I could exercise restraint. Remember, old folks use to say, "Leave it in the hands of the Lord. Whatever the Lord decides is what I would do."

My daughter has to know what the world is really like. She has to know what you can do and what you can't do. It's my job to teach her.

Following up on his response, I chose to approach a sensitive issue that I recalled from the panel discussion. I noted T.I. said that in reference to some of his lyrics he would tell his daughter, "that daddy's making money; it's about a paycheck." My question was how he would respond if his daughter came up and said, "I want to strip or do something illegal because it's about the paycheck."

> First of all, I didn't just say that 'it's about the paycheck.' I said that is Daddy's job, and you can't compare what I do with something illegal. Rap isn't illegal, but as far as that other thing, I'd tell her that "Girls are special." I'd tell her that I've worked this hard so that you don't have to do anything like that.

I apologized to T.I. explaining there are a lot of teen girls emulating the negative images they see on television and hear in music. I asked T.I. where he feels the responsibility lies when these actions are carried out by teens at home, in school and in the community.

> I am an interactive parent. You strengthen your relationships through communication. I have a seven-year- old daughter. When you are looking at her, she is an angel, but when you turn your head, she's just BAD. I let my daughter know that girls are special and boys know that.

> As parents, we should monitor our daughter's interaction with her male relationships and I believe I will, but, if you squeeze soap too tight, it will slip out of your hand. I will monitor my sons more closely.

As we wrapped up the conversation, I wanted to know who some of his female role models were, and what final thoughts did he want to express for his sisters.

> I'd have to say my mother and grandmother. They were strong and independent women who motivated me to be the best that I could be. They would be good role models for others, because they would encourage girls

to believe in themselves, to put family first, to have self-respect and to reach for their goals.

All women need to respect themselves. No one will respect you if you don't respect yourself. You have to treat yourself the way you want to be treated. Women are the origin of life. They are the backbone of the world. Remember girls are special.

REFLECTION PERIOD

REFLECTION PERIOD

College Rape Statistics

- 25% of college women have been victims of rape.
- 8.5% of college men admit to sexually abusing women - but don't consider that rape.
- Of the women who were raped, only 25% described it as rape.
- Of the women who were raped, only 10% reported the assault.
- 47% of the rapes were by dates and romantic acquaintances.

~Sources include RAINN, University of South Florida, Federal Bureau of Investigation (Uniform Crime Statistics, 1996), the U.S. Dept. of Justice, Violence against Women (Bureau of Justice Statistics, the U.S. Dept. Of Justice

To Whom It May Concern:

I have always been proud of my daughter's
independent streak. I just knew that
her sharp mind and sense of self would
carry her far in life. I had no idea
that infatuation and the blind pursuit
of a wealthy fraternity brother and pro-
potential athlete would derail her future.

It seems that she met him at a Greek party
and from that moment set aside her better
judgment in an effort to land what she saw
as a prize catch. I heard about him during
one of her weekly calls home. She carried
on about how nice he was and how she could
not wait to introduce us.

As a former athlete and alumni member of
the same fraternity, I reminded my daughter
to be careful and maintain her grades and
independence. She laughed and told me that
I was being overprotective. She claimed he
was different than most boys. I chose not
to pursue an argument, but now I wonder if
things would have been different for her if
I had.

You see, I received a call from one of her
friends about my daughter being assaulted
and being afraid to tell me about it. I
immediately drove up to the college and
found her dorm room.

As soon as my daughter opened the door and
saw me, she broke down crying. I pulled
her into a hug and let her release the

tears. After regaining her composure, she shared what happened to her.

It seems this brother had been pressuring her to have sex. That fateful night started with her deciding to do it so she wouldn't lose him. They met at his frat house and initially spent their time hanging out in the game room.

As the evening passed, they went up to his room to make out and eventually have sex. As they were laying in bed afterwards, her boyfriend got up saying he would be back in a minute. Caught up in the afterglow and minor discomfort of her first time, she just smiled and continued to lay there in the dark.

She heard the door open and assumed he had returned. When my daughter realized there was more than one set of footsteps, she began to panic and reach for her clothes. "Relax baby. If you want to be with me, you're going to have to be willing to share," the boy laughed, stroking her leg and pressing her against the bed. "This is just part of being with me. Don't you want to please me?"

At that point, I am furious and confused as to why my beautiful and intelligent daughter didn't whoop his ass with the higher level of martial arts training she has. "Daddy, I really thought he loved me," she said with tear-stained cheeks. "I didn't want to lose him."

So after several of his fraternity brothers had finished robbing my daughter of her innocence, she just lay in the bed crying uncontrollably. Her "boyfriend" had never been in the room with his friends, and he also never came back up to hold her or even just talk to her.

In fact once my daughter was able to compose herself, get dressed and go back downstairs, she was shocked to see him sitting on the couch just laughing and drinking. She told me that the boy did not even bother to look at her when she sat next to him and asked, "Why are you ignoring me?"

"Because if you really loved me, you would not have slept with my frat brothers," he said loudly enough for the room to hear. "It's over because I am not going to be with a slut."

Right then, my daughter learned the lesson I had been trying to teach all her life. She had given up her independence and also allowed this boy to disrespect her flagrantly. As much as his words and actions hurt, she was able to get up and leave without crying, but once she got back to her dorm, she broke down and confided in her sorority sister. It was the same sister who had called me.

I continued hugging her and told her we would do what we could. Initially I chose to handle it internally with my fraternity

council. Despite the legal ramifications, I
did not want to bring negative attention to
all of my brothers because of the actions
of a few knuckleheads. I also did not want
my daughter to suffer the humiliation of a
public trial.

The whole situation is still playing
out, but in the meantime, my daughter is
bearing the burden of being an outcast.
Once a popular sorority sister, she now
hears whispers behind her back. When
the boys do approach, they do not show
the respect of courtship, instead they
blatantly come to her thinking that she
will just put it out freely.

I am worried about her, because she seems
to be losing focus in class. I also have
noticed that her weekly calls are turning
into every other week or once a month. When
I asked her about it, she just says that
she's been busy.

Lord, I pray for your guidance. How can
I reach out to my daughter in order to
help her heal? I know there is nothing too
great for you to handle, and I ask for your
healing hands to mend my daughter's heart.
Lord, I also ask for your forgiveness for
the anger and spite that I feel towards
everybody that is hurting my daughter.

To all who are reading this letter now,
I want you to hug your children and let
them know how much you love them. Even if
they are not going through anything, it so

important that they ALWAYS know that you love them and will try to protect them the best you can.

My daughter will survive this, and I will do what I can to be there through it all for her.

Sincerely,

A Vigilant Father

"Do not give away any percent of your will."

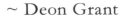

~ Deon Grant

As women with children, especially those married or dating an athlete (past or present), we know that we have to do it all: be a mother, an understanding wife or girlfriend, and of course, we must keep up with sports of our significant other. Deon Grant is an all-star NFL Safety, currently playing for the Seattle Seahawks, and was another member of the celebrity panel at the first annual "Saving Our Daughters" event.

As a single-parent father of a 10-year-old daughter, Deon expressed his continued devotion and the pride of raising his daughter inspired by what he learned from his mother. His mother was a single woman that raised Deon by herself. She spent her life showing him how to respect women and learn how to become a great father.

The world is full of "Baby Mama" Drama involving women that work to deceitfully trap professional athletes through the lure of sexual conquest. They are known as "groupies," and they are predators of sex, fame and money. With so many stories of athletes that have fallen prey to these women, our conversation started with Deon's personal definition of a groupie.

A groupie is someone who tries to ride the coat-tails of who they are following. They associate themselves with that person for what they can get and even if nothing will come out of it. A lot of people think when they see entertainers and athletes that that is the only time groupies show up.

9-to-5 people have groupies too. There are female groupies. There are male groupies. Males can have other male groupies. I can be a groupie for a beautiful female. She doesn't have to be an actress. She can just be walking on the street, or on the sidewalk in a movie shoot. I think a groupie is just a person that falls head-over-heels for a person just because of what that person does.

We wondered what he would tell with his daughter and her friends to avoid becoming groupies themselves.

Well, I'm going to make sure my daughter has everything she wants in life. There is a difference between a groupie and a fan. Some people truly respect what you do. That's a fan, and my daughter will be a fan.

As we further discussed Groupies, Deon spoke about some of his expectations that a young lady should have for herself, her family, her community, etc?

She should require the things that she needs out of life. She needs to be certain that she's not receiving anything that's not of quality. If a young lady has that type of mentality, she's going to be that type of lady that a lot of other young ladies can follow on a positive path.

At the same time, I think she should expect her family to love her for the person she is. That she doesn't have to put on a different face for her family and her community. Let her be herself.

Being a single parent father in the NFL and surrounded by so many distractions, we asked what true respect feels and looks like to him. We also asked him to describe what real love feels and looks like, and whether he felt that someone could have real love without having true respect?

Respect looks and feels like a person really caring about you and your feelings. They honor their word, and they are not putting on a different face for that person. It makes you feel real good inside because you know you have this individual on your side.

Love is something that you are dealing with another individual. Let's see, you are dealing with another individual and you are not trying to bend over backwards for that person. You are not trying to impress that person by being someone other than yourself.

They are doing everything they are supposed to do, and they are not looking to just get something from you. That's what you call real love, and that's how you can tell when a person really loves you. I think you definitely need both. You can respect somebody and not love them, but you definitely need to respect them if are going to truly love the individual. I can only love you if I respect you.

Deon offered this advice to the daughters who do not have a father at home.

Respect yourself. That's the main thing, and you should never accept less than 100% respect. That goes for your body too. Save yourself for the right person. Respect yourself in everything you do. In order for someone to respect you the way they should, you must have the utmost respect for yourself.

As we wrapped up the conversation, Deon shared his thoughts on how having a positive and a strong male role model can positively affect a girl's self-esteem.

When you have that positive male role model she can see how she should be treated. She can go to him for advice. With self-esteem, he can show her that she doesn't have to put herself out there. He allows her to feel good about herself.

REFLECTION PERIOD

REFLECTION PERIOD

INTERMISSION

T.I. devoting time for the parents in his neighborhood.

Deon, T.I. and Sean took time to speak with teen girls and single parent mothers at the "Saving Our Daughters" panel during the summer of 2008.

Anwan giving hugs at It's Cool To Be Smart Toy Giveaway for deserving little girls in his home town in Washington D.C. for Christmas 2007.

LOBBY TALK

"One of the greatest gifts that GOD ever gave to man was a woman, and by honoring women, we honor The Father."

- Nappy Roots

"A young lady should expect unconditional love for herself from herself, for her family and community, self-discipline, healthy boundaries in her dealings with the opposite sex. She should have an insatiable desire to learn, an unyielding love of GOD and a desire to serve others.

From her family, she should expect unconditional love, support, guidance, encouragement, laughter and a beautiful sense of belonging, acceptance, and security. She should also expect to be challenged cerebrally and inspirationally. Lastly, her family should make her feel like she can do anything she sets her mind to.

From her community, she should expect respect because she'll carry herself in a manner that will 'oh so humbly' demand it."

- Chad L. Coleman, from HBO's Award-Winning Show The Wire

"Affirm your daughter daily. Build up her confidence at home so the world will not be able to break her down. If she never hears from anyone else that she is beautiful, smart or capable, she should know she is all of those things because she hears it from you everyday. Speak into her life until you see her blossom into the strong, intelligent, empowered woman she was destined to become. Even when she begins to walk with her head held high, continue to affirm your daughter. "

- Lisa Wu Hartwell from Bravo's "Real Housewives of Atlanta"

"My mother is like a money market bank account I can deposit anything into (her), and expect to yield a high interest return. I am the person I am today and the man I will eventually become because of my mom. Your parents are like royalty. Would you ever expect a court jester to disrespect the royal king and queen of the land?"

- Doc Shaw, 16, "Malik" from "Tyler Perry House of Payne"

LOBBY TALK

"As a parent, it is important to realize that the example you set is the example your kids will follow."

- Gary Owen, Actor/Comedian | BET Comic View

"In life, as women we are sometimes forced into situations that can on the outside seem to victimize us as well as characterize us as defeated. In that moment you feel helpless, powerless, and minute compared to the GIANT that you are fighting against. I want to challenge young ladies to FEEL and HEAL and take back your power. As a victim of abuse myself, I can tell you that it is a process, but what helped me get past it was something that I was told: No matter what has happened in your life, no matter the road blocks, the GIANTS that may come against you. Order your life the way you see it. Just like looking at a menu when you sit down at a restaurant, you tell the waitress "I want a turkey burger, no onions, extra cheese, no mayo," and if she brings you something else, you send it back. THAT is how you should view your entire life. Set a goal. Make a plan and DECIDE that no matter what adversity you may face that it WILL not, CANNOT affect my destiny."

- Treynce from the 2nd Season of Fox's American Idol

"We need to first teach our daughters to be financially independent. Allow them to make their financial mistakes at home. Let them learn to pay for their own credit cards, car notes, gas, and bills while still at home. When it is finally time for our girls to leave home, they should 1) be able to understand how much they have to spend on extracurricular activities. 2) be able to move into their own home. 3) be financially independent. It builds self esteem and self security."

- Bone Crusher & His Wife Aneesah

"As mothers, it is important to know that we must take responsibility in our role and not expect society to raise our daughters. We must always prepare our daughters for the trials and tribulations that they will encounter in life and let them know that no matter what; we are on their side and understand."

- Erin Baxter, The Recording Academy Atlanta

"Stay focused on your path and everything will fall into place."

- Grammy Award Winner Ne-Yo

How can we discuss positive ways of communicating when it relates to my mother's boyfriend?

If my daughter is uncomfortable with my significant other, should we include him in trying to work out the situation?

I am a single mother in my mid-twenties. I am having trouble with my girls putting pressure on me concerning dating older men. Is this something that I should bring up to their father?

_____

_____

_____

_____

_____

_____

_____

_____

_____

_____

_____

_____

I am a single parent mother, and I am having financial difficulty but have received some support from my ex. What are your feelings on taking our Black men to court for Child Support and pressuring them to provide full support?

If we feel our mothers are not being responsible as a parent, do we have an obligation to seek advice from our fathers even if they are in another relationship?

I have been out of the dating scene for five years, what advice would you give single parent mothers stepping back into the dating arena?

How do you feel fathers should educate us as young girls about young men?

How soon should single parent mothers plan to introduce their daughters to men they are very interested in?

As daughters, how should we communicate with our fathers if we do not approve of his new relationship?

As men in your relationships where you are not the father, what is your take on disciplining the mother's daughter?

I am 16-years-old and ready to be sexually active. How do I share this with my mother?

My daughter is ready to be sexually active, how do I effectively express the importance of waiting when I know she is going to do it regardless of what I tell her?

If I was sexually assaulted by someone I didn't know, how do I talk to my parents about the fact that I kind of enjoyed it?

My daughter is having a hard time excepting her stepfather. He has been nothing but nice to her and great to me, and when I have asked her why she doesn't like him, she responds that "I just DON'T!" My daughter is everything to me, how do I work this situation out?

My mother let her husband abuse me so she could continue to live a fabulous lifestyle. Also their daughter together has been provided a great lifestyle, and I seemed to get the short end of the stick. How do I confront my mother about this now that I am an adult?

My daughter is pregnant again for the 4th time, and she is only 23 with no job and no education! As a mother, how I do handle this, because I feel like I have failed as a mother.

Tyler Perry actor Gary Sturgis speaks on 97.5 PRAISE about Saving Our Daughters during Domestic Violence Month.

From Good Boys to Good Men: Deon with Tyrik (11) and Juwuan (10) sons of Actress, Radio & TV Personality Tangie Larkin (V-103 Atlanta).

Gary Sturgis teams up with Radio Personality Greg Street, Scales and Skinny of Nappy Roots to speak at a high school in Atlanta on respecting women.

ACT II

"My mother told me I was blessed, and I have always taken her word for it. Being born from- or reincarnated from- royalty is nothing like being blessed. Royalty is inherited from another human being; blessedness comes from God."

~ Duke Ellington

To Whom It May Concern:

My dear mother, I am writing this letter to you to thank you for your love and support through all of our circumstances. I didn't realize what we really had when we had it, but I do now. Mother you said that I was strong enough and smart enough to make it through any situation, through anything, and while I said "Okay, Mother," I didn't really understand it then. I want you to know that now I do.

As a child, I watched what you did for us and how you took care of me and my brother. You always knew and did what needed to be done. When you worked because you felt that 'we' needed it, I acknowledge it now. When you didn't explore your youthful environment the way someone else would, I didn't see you as wasting your opportunities, I saw you only as my mother.

My love for you and my respect for what you taught me, only increases daily. There is no day that I don't reflect on something you told me. There is no day that I don't recognize that with your words and actions you knew that I was going to be exactly where I am now. I am successful, more successful than I could have ever imagined. More opportunities than I would have ever expected. I am the man that I am because of you. I am the man that my son deserves because of you.

I love and appreciate you more than I can ever express. I just wish that the love, the respect and the joy that I have in my heart for you could be expressed to you as fully as I feel it. I know that God is in control of everything, but I wish I could have just one more moment on this earth with you. I wish I could have one more conversation with you or another opportunity to feel your touch. Mother I am a reflection of you, and hopefully, I am one-tenth of you. Always, always, always know that you are in my heart and in my soul.

Sincerely,

A Beloved Son and Father

"Inspect what you expect."

~ Sean Garrett

Mr. Sean Garrett is a soft-spoken, multi-talented Grammy songwriter who has written for just about every major musical artist under the sun. The list of inspiring artists he has written for includes Beyoncé, Fergie (from the Black Eye Peas), Chris Brown, Ciara, Usher and Enrique Iglesias just to name a few. Sean has also joined these artists as a talented singer and has released some songs setting off strong sexual overtones with women.

After recently watching one of these steamy videos, I chose to lead the conversation off by asking what women inspired him to become the man he is, as well as the influence they have had on his relationships with women.

> Let me see, my mother is number one. I would also say my mom's sisters. Then I would have to go abroad, because there are quite a few who have influenced me like Coretta Scott King.

> My mother is number one, because in my eyes, she is a great representative of what a real woman is. My mother was from the South, and she struggled as a young woman trying to find herself, especially coming from a family of 10. She, her brothers and sisters were kind of split up when they were young, so they pretty much had to find their way.

My mom had two sons. She worked really hard to make a way for me and my brother until she married my dad, but she taught me so many things about being resilient, being smart, learning from other peoples' mistakes, and instead of being a talker she taught me to be more of a listener.

Through her examples, she always gave and instilled in me an unstoppable drive. No matter what, she taught me to never stop, to always stretch and reach for my dreams. I lost my mom like five years ago and losing her amplified everything that she ever told me.

It's just funny when you lose someone that you cared about so much and who had so much influence in your life. My mother was someone that every day something that she said sticks out in my mind. It kind of gives me the ability to move forward in my day and continue to be the best I can.

Coretta Scott King was such a beautiful strong woman. She sort of showed me what being a real wife was about, as well as showing me what being a strong black woman is about. She also personifies what being a great team player is.

She taught me so many different things. A lot of women probably could not go through seeing their husband go through what hers did; she saw him go through the challenges of his whole struggle. She was always the rock that gave him the ability to be all that he could be.

Given the inspiration that his mother provided, I wondered about his opinion of women from her generation compared to the women of his own generation?

I think these women [my mother and Coretta Scott

King] would be great role models for young ladies today because they had a sense of knowing who they were, they stood for something and they would not allow a friend or what everyone else was doing affect who they were.

I feel like my generation tends to not be focused. They are misled by a lot of things that don't really matter. It's all material things. Not to take anything away from the women of my generation, I just feel like the women that I looked up to were sounder with who they were and where they were going.

They displayed a great sense of beauty by carrying themselves as real women. You know what I mean, they were still beautiful, they were still dainty and they were elegant; but at the same time, they didn't have to display it in a way that was over the top. You still got the sense that they were real women and that they could do anything and everything that any other woman could do, but they just did it in a real classy way.

The conversation then transitioned to his expectations of what he thinks a young lady should have in relation to herself, her family and her community.

I think she should inspect what she expects. That's always been my point of view. If you expect a lot from your community, you need to find out what goes on in your community. You know what I mean, you've got to be exhaustive; you've got to learn about your community. It's the same thing in relationships, and it's the same thing with choosing a man.

You can't expect respect from a man who has never been respectful to women. You know what I'm saying. You can't meet a man in a place that most people would think is the wrong place. I think you've got to inspect what you expect in life.

You make things difficult when it's not. You want a good man, so you go to a club to find him? It depends on what you want. If you're young and vibrant and you want some excitement, you go to the club. You're definitely going to find it there.

If you want a more laid back relationship, you might not want to choose that guy you met in the club. You might want to choose the guy you met, I don't know, perhaps at the bank. That's not to say that all guys that work at a bank or in a corporate setting are better than anyone else. I'm just saying you may have a better chance with him.

During the "Saving Our Daughters Panel," I had noted that Sean said that he could not be held responsible for all of his lyrics because of all the people he writes for. I asked him if he could put that in context for us?

Yeah, I mean, everything is relative. Like that's how I have to look at it. All of my intentions are honorable, and if you know Sean Garrett, you know my heart is pure. It's pure with love, and I'm speaking from a place of fun, love, life, positivity and energy.

Being young you know that I want to speak about things that are going on. Or to talk about things we consider fun. You know that when you succeed at 18 years old there are so many things that you consider fun that your parents don't.

It's probably 80% of the things that your parents feel like you're bugging. You don't need to be thinking of that, or you don't need to be doing that. The perspective is always different. I can only think as a songwriter. If I am writing a love song, it is going to speak from my generation's perspective, and the generation might think that might be something that needs to be said.

At the same time, who am I to say anything about the things that they said when they were 15 or 16 or 17 years old. A lot of the songs that I write are specifically written for people depending on where they are in their life. You have to understand, because the same pet that you keep can be the same pet that bites you.

What I mean by that is you can get caught up in a situation where you write only love songs, right, and I mention those from a songwriter's point of view. You may be a great writer of love songs, but in order to survive in this industry you've got to do all kinds of songs. Be it party songs, club songs, rap songs, happy songs, sad songs, and great songs.

To be able to survive, you have to do what the economy calls for you to do to survive. So I said that to say that all of the music and lyrics that I write are coming from a good place. Maybe, sometimes, every now and then the lyrics are a little bit racy depending on the artist.

Given that there are so many young women growing up without a positive father figure in the household, I wanted to know what advice Sean had about these girls finding positive role models.

To find a role model you respect and that you can look up to. You don't necessarily have to interact with them, but you could study them. You could do that by reading about them, or watch how they treat people around them.

Look at someone who carries themselves the way you would like to carry yourself when you grow up. They are all around you. You don't have to have just one specific role model. You can have a great deal of them.

One could be an actor, a teacher, a coach, a pastor, or even an artist. You don't always have to view their negative side. You can study their positive side. To me it's elementary. Life is what you've got in your head.

If you want to be real intricate, then you should study intricate people. If you want to go to a great school, start working towards it now. Start getting involved in activities that will lead you down the road to where you want to go. You can't play around for half of your life then decide at 15 that you want to go to college.

Keep great models in front of you. I think the "Saving Our Daughters" forum was phenomenal, and I think we should do it on a bigger scale. Instead of having 300 or 100 girls in the room, we should have 5000 in the room. I think this is the way.

Communicating with people is the only way we can help each other; by us exchanging information. Everyone who has made it from Denzel Washington to Michael Jackson, we all needed someone. We've all learned from someone. I think Michael Jackson learned from James Brown.

Straight up, I have studied Lionel Richie, I have studied Neyo and I have studied Michael Jackson. We all have to learn from someone. Anyone successful walking around, created the will for themselves.

This is the best thing I think I do to help in urban communities, because the only way to affect their lives in a strong manner is to encourage girls to interact with people that they consider successful and that they will listen to.

He continued with these words for girls moving into womanhood.

I just want to give the message to my sisters to continue to believe in them themselves, and I can't say that enough. Just continue to believe in yourself, and you've got to believe in God. You've got to believe that He put you here for a reason.

Being positive is half the battle, I swear it is. I've been broke, and I've been in situations where I didn't know what I was going to do. I'm just being real, and it's just about being positive. I never doubted God, never.

I've been scared sometimes, and I don't know why God wanted me to be so candid with you. I really care about these young girls, little boys and girls. I really try to connect with organizations like yours, and I'm really proud to be a part of It's Cool To Be Smart.

As we wrapped up the conversation, I decided that I could not let Sean go without asking him the ultimate question. If he was single and looking, what qualities would the woman need to have?

Um, a warm heart, a true warm heart. I think that it starts with a warm heart, and you can tell when you first meet someone. You can just feel it. You know I'm a Pisces, so I'm kind of intuitive. I just want someone who has a warm heart and that cares about love, life, feeling and that is not cold.

I'm just not attracted to a cold heart. So you know that's

the first thing that kind of turns on a light for me, and
I know I'm giving away some jewels (Laughter). Of
course the woman doesn't know that when I meet her.
A person will come at you and they'll be as nice to you
as they want to be, that doesn't necessarily mean they
have a warm heart or they have a loving spirit.

For me, they just have to have a joyfulness about
themselves. That's what I like, and I think love is
elementary. It's like the first grade I mean.
What's your name? It's such and such. Can we play
together? You know what I'm saying. Do you want
to play on the monkey bars with me? I don't feel, it's
about how much money you're making, or how you're
living, no matter what level you're living on; at the end
of the day, life is still, elementary.

You make life more difficult when you make it college.
It's simple, you respect me and I respect you. You love
me and I love you. Yeah, you have mishaps, but I think
when you have that opportunity, you can't make a
mistake.

The first time you have that opportunity, show them
love from that first moment. It could be a killer; it
could be the worst person in the world. If you greet
them with love, it's going to be real difficult for them to
have a problem with you. At least that's what I think.

REFLECTION PERIOD

REFLECTION PERIOD

"You made all the delicate, inner parts of my body and knit me together in my mother's womb."

- Psalm 139:13

To Whom It May Concern:

Your mother and I just left the doctor's office. Today we found out that we are having a daughter. I was hoping my first child would be a son, but on the ride home, I realize how excited I am about your arrival in a few months.

I am thrilled that the Lord has blessed us with your presence. At the same time, I am terrified about being responsible for a beautiful new mind. You will find out that the world can be a scary place, but I will ALWAYS do what I can to protect and prepare you for it.

When you are little, I will give you piggyback rides, have tickle fights and read silly books with you. I will teach you how to ride a bike, kick a soccer ball, play baseball and try to provide you as many opportunities for a great childhood that I can. At the same time, I will teach you how to respect yourself and others.

As you get a bit older, you will become interested in boys, so I will constantly strive to be the best man I can. I will do this so you will be able to recognize how a good man should behave. I will also probably drive you crazy as a protective father, but I promise that I will NEVER abandon you.

I know that eventually you will meet a man that you recognize as your soul mate. I will pray that I have equipped you with the ability to recognize the difference between love and lust when that day comes. When the time comes for me to walk you down the aisle, I will take comfort in knowing that you will always be my little girl.

Sincerely,

A Loving Father

"A father has to have a consistent relationship with his daughter."

~ Lamman Rucker

My sisters hold on to your seats. In *Tyler Perry's Why Did I Get Married* and *Tyler's Perry's Meet the Browns*, this phenomenal young brother clearly showed how black men should be respecting their women. Sitting down for our conversation, he discussed how influential the women in his life have been, the importance of communication, and how he has applied life lessons into his work as an actor amongst other things.

The conversation started by discussing Lamman's role (Sheriff Troy) in *Tyler Perry's Why Did I Get Married*. As a woman, I personally was impressed with his character's understanding of Sheila's (played by actress Jill Scott) plight, and how Sheriff Troy helped to move her from the negative relationship. I wondered where he developed the understanding from, and what his feelings about women can overcoming similar situations.

I think I got that from being a good listener. It's a combination of the friends I have, the women I've listened to and the relationships I've been in. I was listening to her instead of judging her, and how accountable she needs to be about being in the relationship she was in.

I also learned by just listening to women that have

found themselves in situations like that. Instead of judging them, you have to listen to them and help them work through what they need to for themselves to move forward from a situation or from a relationship that might not be good for them.

I've had people close to me go through some very similar challenges. It was about learning how to talk to them, just listening to them, and trying to figure out what are the dynamics and how did this happen?

I just learned that there is a certain amount of love and nurturing that needs to happen, but there is a certain way you need to move and challenge people to demand that if they want something different they have to make the decision to find it within themselves to change things. That was also modeled by my father. So as a man, I was fortunate enough to have another man model for me what good listening and good communication was. I've also got a wonderful mother that is a great communicator, and I've had some training. Those are the things that I tried to apply to the character.

You play such patient men, and you mentioned the art of listening. What advice would you give parents and their children about this skill?

I think that goes back to communication. I think most people talk, but they don't really listen. I also think listening is a combination. It is not only just listening with your ears, but listening with your mind and your heart. If you don't have that sensibility, you are going to lose a lot of battles.

There will be a lot of communications that you are not successful with. I learned how to be very attentive and patient. I am not being selfish, and I am not trying to win a conversation. I am trying to make sure I'm patient and be really astute to what someone is really going through. How they feel and what they're thinking. What the challenge may be to them even having this conversation.

I have to do it without making assumptions. Why haven't we talked about this, this and that? Instead of judging that young person or telling them that you know better than them. When you respect the intelligence of the other person, you are going to get more from them, and more out of them. I think parents don't dignify the pride, the ego and the level of self-assurance that a young person has and sometimes talk down to them.

Of course, I am very much an advocate of the parent is the parent and the child is the child, but when you are really working on a strong relationship and strong communication, you have to have strong listening skills and be the one who models that as the adult.
You are teaching that child how to communicate and listen by being a good listener. It's something that a parent has to work to do. It's nothing that you can assume that a parent is going to have. Listening is how you learn. Listening is how you get more information.

As we talked about communicating with kids, I asked at what age parents should start teaching them that the world is an unfair place.

You know that's tough, that's one of those things where I think parents are the ones who have to make that decision. That's a decision that really relates to how soon we choose to show. When do we choose to start allowing our child to lose their innocence so to speak? I think that varies. I've seen that happen in different ways at different times for so many people, and there are ways that it works and ways that it doesn't.

I would say for me it's been to my advantage that I learned significantly early on that the world can be unforgiving. I will say that as a man that I think I've suffered the consequences of being with a woman who has been sheltered for quite some time. It was a long time before she had the rude awakening that the world can be a very unforgiving place, and she wasn't equipped with the defense mechanisms to cope and deal with what that really means. I would say that that was one of the things that men are sometimes most responsible for.

Sometimes they protect and cuddle the girls, and if anything I feel like that's more of a mother's job. You know for a girl, and that's where the balance comes in. I think mothers nurture their sons and discipline their daughters, and fathers nurture their daughters and discipline their sons. So what the perfect age is I have no idea (laughter). I think that most of the time these things kind of happen randomly.

Their environment kind of does it before the parent or parents deliberately say "Oh, here's a news flash," or "Get ready." I think that's probably what everyone needs to get prepared for. How do you then serve a young person's questions or manage them once they've been hurt, or once they've had that significant experience?

You know, that's the first time they are slapped in the face with that kind of reality. I find that that's what people are most unprepared for. Parents are often at times least prepared for how to respond to these moments. I don't know if it's always a parent's job, or my job as a role model, to say, "Let me show you what's really going on."

Sometimes you can ruin a child's self-esteem and scare the hell out of them (laughter). You want them to be hopeful and positive about their future, but it's going to have to have some balance. I don't want to cuss, but once the shit hits the fan, the best teachers and parents are the ones that actually can facilitate the child learning how to deal with that process so they can interpret it and move on from it.

I asked him what he thought is most detrimental, an absent father or a mother that makes bad decisions? By bad decisions, I clarified that I meant the mother bringing men in and out of their lives.

I hate to walk the fence about some of this stuff, but I firmly disagree with pointing fingers, especially when we are looking at one specific area. I think that it's absolutely a combination of these two factors. I can't say that just having a father around is the way it should be, because it shouldn't be if that man is not a good man and/or not a good father. I mean that's just as bad as not being with the child's natural father and bringing some weak man around.

It's not good for her and not good for her family, because I don't see that being any different. So obviously having a good father figure around, whether it is in the home or in direct proximity to the family, is always going to be important to young girls. We significantly underestimate a father's role in the development of young girls, and I think it's extremely important and highly instrumental to a woman having the full perspective of the world.

The relationship she has with her father has something to do with the relationship she's going to have with other males throughout her life personally and professionally. I don't know whether or not I'd point the finger in one direction or the other, because it really is a combination of the two. I would definitely say it starts with a father making the decision to be there and be present, and even if he's not in the home, he needs to make the commitment to having a very strong, open, honest, disciplined and consistent relationship with his daughter. Mothers have to allow that to happen.

I know many of situations where it's the mother of those daughters that are actually the barrier to the relationship between the daughter and father, because of their relationship with the man. They don't allow that to happen, because they think, "I'm a woman, and I can raise this little girl on my own." I think this is a very real misconception.

During all of my conversations for this book, I have asked the men about who their personal heroes have been and Lamman shared this.

Well, I would start with the women in my family, in particular my mother's mother Wilhemina Brown. Once I came to realize that she herself was a college graduate, you know, it really kind of sunk in. It really exemplified a love for an excellence of achievement in my family.

She was always the symbol for me in our family to reach for what you expect, and it was interesting to have that odyssey two generations away from me. All three of her daughters, my mother and aunts are all highly accomplished women as well, both artistically and academically. So I think my grandmother was the person that exemplified that the most for me.

She was a teacher as well and taught for over 40 years. She was one of those people that kids or other people would come by or send her things. They would call or get in touch with her. They would come by with their kids because they were students of hers since grade school.

How they use to hold her so dear to their hearts because

she was there for them and she was that teacher that they never forgot. The one that made such a significant impression on them, and then she maintained contact with them.

So it's kind of weird, I've always noticed these things and some of the things she use to do with me. She used to send me stuff in the mail like educational quizzes. I remember this little thing that use to come in the Sunday paper, Johnny Wonder or something like that, and it had everything from word scrambles to trivia questions. There were math and geography kind of questions, and the Encyclopedia Brown book series. It was just all kinds of stuff that didn't really significantly hit me until later.

It was just how much she influenced me personally. By her being a teacher, an academic and incredible woman, but also embraced the arts. She was one of those season subscribers to the opera, to the ballet, and things like that. So my grandmother would probably be my most significant personal hero.

He went on further to tell me why his grandmother would be such a great role model for young girls and women today.

She was highly involved and very philanthropic in her community. She started community leadership groups, a mothers group she founded. A few of these women became known as 'Auntie So-and-so' in my life, but were really women from her groups. They were her personal and professional peers. They accomplished great things like Master degrees and PhD's. I think that those are all very important things to do and model.

Not just for young women but for young men also. I would say some of the things to focus on are to get their education and continue to further your education. Complete all levels of your education, and then go on into the field that you've trained yourself in and prepared yourself for. Excel at that, and really be able to touch people.

Have a strong peer group, because my grandmother had mentors and she mentored a lot of people. She was very active in the community, in the church and always gave back to her community. She was very passionate about being vested in her family. I loved her very much, and it was very evident that she loved me as well. She was vested in me, my brother, my sister and my cousins. There were also a variety of other people she was vested in. She was definitely one of those people that everybody else's kids were her kids too, and I found that's an example of a woman's worth.

That's an example for young women to follow. They should definitely handle their own homes, but good people and good models also set examples for others.

As we finished off our conversation, I asked Lamman what he would look for in a mate if he were single and available.

Honestly the things I talked about already. I am looking for someone like my grandmother and the type of woman she was. I mean that's my standard. All of those things are what I think is what a woman should be. I'm looking for a renaissance woman just like I consider myself to be a renaissance man.

I am looking for someone who's trying to develop themselves. I want her to be a very balanced person, because I appreciate a woman who is a woman of the new millennium. I like a woman who is very accomplished and is about getting her act together and accomplishing her goals, and being someone who is assertive enough to redefine what a woman is.

I do still appreciate a woman having a traditional role, but sometimes women don't seem to have that. I know sisters who don't know how to manage a family at all.

They do not know how to do any of the traditional roles of a woman, and of course there are plenty of men who don't know how to treat them as traditional men use to be as well.

I'm not trying to come off as chauvinistic. I really do appreciate a woman that can balance between the ability to be the domestic woman and the ability and vision to be whatever the new age millennium woman is. I love a woman who is educated, has traveled and has visions and goals. I know some extremely dynamic women.

I want a woman who is as fully evolved as she can be, and she's doing the best to reach her full potential whatever that may be because that is going to be a different thing for everybody. My mother is a scholar, an author and a revolutionary, not to mention that she is also a dancer, a mother and a grandmother.

I'm interested in a woman who is interested in being everything she can be, and that's really what that is. My goal is to find out what my potential is and to put the work in that will maximize that potential.

REFLECTION PERIOD

REFLECTION PERIOD

"For this cause shall a man leave his father and mother, and shall be joined unto his wife, and they two shall be one flesh."

- Ephesians 5:31

To Whom It May Concern:

My parents gave me one of the greatest gifts I could have ever received from them, and it's so interesting that until that gift was altered, I never recognized nor respected the enormity of what God had granted me through my parents.

Paul and Elizabeth married long before I came into the world. My parents were married 19 years and had 9 children prior to my birth. My dad, who had to drop out of high school, took care of 10 children by working three jobs and sometimes four. My mom who also did not finish high school stayed at home with us.

Growing up we didn't have a lot of money and were actually considered poor, but I never knew that. What I did know was that I had two parents who loved us all and loved each other. With that love we also received guidance, compassion, strength and so many more qualities that I can't remember them all. My parents sent us all to college somehow, and somehow we all graduated.

The sweetest gift I received was seeing the love affair between my parents. No, it was not always easy nor was it always pleasant, but through all of it they stayed together and raised their family together.

They were to renew their vows for their 50th wedding anniversary. Unfortunately, my dad had a heart attack two weeks before the wedding date, and he was bedridden until he passed away quietly at home four months later with his 'Lizzy' by his side. She said he was the love of her life, and she would do anything for him because they had agreed 'til death we do part.'

I was allowed to see that and will be eternally grateful for the God given gift of a strong family. My parent-lead family showed me how to be a real father and a real husband in the family that I now lead.

Sincerely,

A Blessed Father

"True respect is when two people can communicate without raising their voices and without going to bed angry."

~ Gary Sturgis

Gary Anthony Sturgis is a New Orleans born actor/writer/director best known for his portrayal of the villain in two of Tyler Perry's biggest hit films, "Diary of A Mad Black Woman" (Jamison Jackson) and "Daddy's Little Girls" (Joseph Woods). He also co-starred opposite Terrence Howard in "Pride", as the charming yet sinister pimp/drug dealer Franklin Washington.

After a brief meeting with *It's Cool To Be Smart* Executive Director, Curtis Benjamin, Gary was happy to contribute to the *Saving Our Daughters* project. Arrangements were made, and we were pleased to sit down and discuss a variety of topics with him.

As we sat down and learned more about him, it was revealed that he had been married 16 years to a woman he has been with for 23 years. This led to a discussion about the alarming rate of failed marriages that continued to be reported in our community. We asked what his plan for correctable action would be.

I'm a living example of correctional action. I came from a family that's still together. My wife and I are still together. We're providing the standard two parent family, and this is what was promised to these kids when we set out to do this.

My mother and father have been together for some 40 odd years and I mean this is all I know. You sort of model yourself after what you see. In my situation, I got to see a set of parents who stuck it out through thick and thin and through hell and high water together. So that's the image of what I saw a family being. Mother stays with father and father stays with mother, and I've kind of got the same thing.

I've got a wife that loves me so unconditionally that it doesn't matter if I'm not working at the moment. "Oh, Gary's career took a slider. Oh I'm out of here." It was never about the success. It was about me and my heart, and when you have a good structure like that you can provide these kids the structure that they need.

Because there are things they are going to learn from both parents. They learn about women from their mothers, and they learn about men from their fathers. They need both of these images. Men have to step up. It doesn't matter if you can't keep the relationship up. What matters is that you provide for these kids, because they're your offspring, and if you don't, they are going to go out into the world and another man will.

It doesn't matter if my girl and I can make it. What does matter is that this offspring that we brought into the world who didn't ask to be here gets the proper guidance so that she/he will make better choices than we did, because obviously at this point we've made some bad choices. I think it's more important for us to realize that our offspring need our guidance especially the young ladies because it's really hard out here.

As we talked about building family relationships, he shared about his own close relationship with his mom and other women role models in his life.

My mom is a fun-loving woman, but she is also a very strong-willed woman. She's a real woman, and she is a very hard working woman. I got a lot of my creativity from my parents. My father use to be a singer, and my mom was a model when I was born. So that image of entertainment was always around me.

I was a good 'A' student, and I was kind of doing a little bit better than my brothers in school. I don't know why, but they were just average in school. I loved school, so it must have had something to do with liking school. I also loved that she be happy when I brought home good grades, and I liked that she liked that. It was motivational to me, and I wanted to keep her smiling and happy and bragging on the fact that I was an 'A' student. It seemed to bring her joy, so I wanted to keep doing it and I did.

The thing that I always loved most about my mother was that she allowed us to have free will. She was about free will, but she would wait to see the kind of choices that we would make. She would be guiding us, but still allowed us to make choices and I was glad for that. I was actually pretty good at making choices. When I chose the theater at 17, a lot of parents were telling their kids, "No, no you need to focus on a real job," they would say "That ain't going to get you nowhere."

You know a lot of kids got that. My mother was 100% behind me once I said I wanted to do it. We didn't have money, and I was barely scraping by to get through college. She was behind me a 100% when I said I wanted to do this thing. It was that kind of love and that kind of belief that inspired me.

I think it's that belief system that has carried on into my parenting. I tell my kids they can be whatever they want to be. I encourage my kids to start thinking about what they want to do after high school now. High school will be over before you know it.

I just try to motivate them to do their own thing in their own time. It's one life to live. It's yours. I can't live it for you. All I can do is help guide you through. They must be happy with their choices. Life is a learning process. Life is not a dress rehearsal. It's a full performance, and sometimes you are going to fall on your face, sometimes you're going to get a standing ovation. You just have to keep going until you find out what you want to do.

I grew up in a house full of guys, and I didn't have a sister. It was interesting being in a household with one woman with a husband and three boys to bring up. She is my first female role model because she taught me a whole bunch about respecting women and about respect in general. That influence was very important to me.

After that, I would say Debbie Allen and Felicia Rashad. When I got into the acting business, Debbie was doing her thing with the show 'Fame,' and that was one of the first shows you got to see a bunch of young, talented people doing their thing where she was such a driving force influencing them to be stronger with what they do.

Later, we would see her sister Rashad doing the Cosby Show. I think both of them painted a picture of strength, pride and independence to young women as well as things at that time that women weren't being taught as much of. It was always follow the leader to some guy, and I think both of them showed a lot of class and poise and talent. In the business I was in, they both were always guiding forces and showed me determination.

As we continued to talk, Gary shared the qualities he looked for when he chose his wife.

Well it goes back to my mom. My family always told me when I was little that you find a woman like your mother. So I wanted qualities like my mother has. I wanted a pretty girl, and she definitely had to be pretty (laughter). Yeah, guys do go for the physical first, so she had to be pretty. She had to be nice, and she had to be a good parent. She had to be someone who could handle kids. I had a younger brother once I went to college, so technically my mother had to deal with four boys.

I wanted a woman who knew how to handle financial business. Being an artist, I'm more into making money, not managing money. So I needed a chick that could handle bank business, and that was really important, because my mom always handled all of the finances. So I had to find a woman who was very good and very talented in handling a bank account, and she had to know how to invest stuff and move money around.

There are just some things I didn't know how to do. I grew up kind of poor so most of my money stayed in my pocket (laughter). Hey, I'm just being real. I never had to learn how to use the bank, because it didn't stay in there long (laughter). I wouldn't even get to go over there, and I knew that because of the business that I was in, I hoped to make a lot of money and I needed to be with someone who knew what to do with a lot of money. So these are the kind of qualities I looked for.

She had to have a kind heart, a warm personality and had to make me laugh. Life is pretty serious in the entertainment business, so I'm ripe for a good laugh. I had to find someone with a good personality and definitely like the president, in this business you have to find someone who complements you and in the business you are in.

Gary offered further in-depth answers about true respect for women; what true love is and what expectations he feels a young lady should have for herself, her family, and her community.

True respect is when two people can communicate without raising their voices and without going to bed angry. It feels and looks like you can go to another person and be open, be you and be real with them.

They'll respect your realness. Sometimes there are things that you have to say that aren't necessarily favorable, and in reverse this person can come back and say this is how I feel about what you did or said. Both of those things can really spring back.

They may not be the warmest things or things we want to hear. True respect is when two people can respect each other's feelings to the point where it doesn't have to get out of hand, violent or verbal. That's what true respect looks like and feels like to me.

Ok, I feel I'm a pretty open person. I've been in love and I've loved before. For me love is unconditional, because there are no conditions. There are no rules, no regulations and no if-then statements. When people say "I'd love you if," that's not real love to me. That's love with conditions.

There are a whole bunch of things that can go wrong in a relationship, and we've been together for 23 years. When you're in a real loving relationship things are going to be rocky sometimes, and it is how well your love survives through this that determines what you have.

For me it has to be unconditional, and if my relationship wasn't unconditional I wouldn't be in the marriage that I'm in. I've been in this relationship for 23 years and married for 16 of them. I look around at all the people that are in the entertainment business and what they're going through. Look at Morgan Freeman, he's getting a divorce and he's 71.

I mean you don't get a divorce at 71. I've been fortunate, and sometimes you just meet the right person. I met my girl in college. It was one of those situations where I met my girl in college, and I used my popular name which at the time was "Batman" with Omega Psi Phi. She said, "Did your mama name you that?" She did not know me (laughter), and I said to myself that this girl could be my wife.

Remember, conditional love comes with degrees. You cannot have unconditional love. I do think it's possible to love someone you don't respect. Respect is something that's earned. It's not something that's given. I've got a couple of family members like that. I don't think it's impossible. I think in relationships it may be weird, but I don't think it's impossible.

Respect is something that is earned. So, if you don't respect them at the moment, you could later. I don't think it is always right to say, "I don't feel respected, so let me ditch you." You have to teach people how to respect you. Some people don't know. I think a lot of people don't know how to respect women.

I've had situations in my life where I have verbally disrespected people including women. I'm not going to be that kind of person to pretend that I've never done that, I'm not going to do that. You learn in time by doing things, and sometimes you have to learn things through trial and error.

You lose so much while doing that, but the goal is if you really love them to try to earn that respect back. In fact, that's where love really kicks in. I do believe you can love someone without respecting them, but it won't last long. Love and respect are like a time released capsule.

I think she should expect the best that the world has to offer in all regards, because you know God put all of these things here and all of these emotions and wonderful things are here for a reason. They're not here just for a reason, and they're not here just for white people or rich people; they're here for all people.

Especially for His people, so I think a young lady should keep God first and hold her head up with respect. This is especially true for African-American women, because it is a lot harder with our community. If they'll remember it's not where you come from, it's not how you start out in life, but it's how you finish. It's how you carry yourself.

They need to realize that everything out here in the world is for them. They can have it, but there are rules and regulations that go with this stuff. It is like the person who gets the best grades is the person that will get better opportunities. Study and always try to do the best you can.

My mother would tell me, "You've got to remember you represent a family. It's not just you when you walk out there. You represent a whole family. The last name that you carry represents a family, and the perception of people in the world of that name will depend on how you carry yourself."

It doesn't matter what stage you are in: poverty, middle class or high class, because it's how you carry yourself. Young women need to understand they have a presence about them, and that they don't even need to open their mouths. It's in the way they walk, and they don't even have to open their mouths.

Read more Maya Angelou books (laughter), and read as much of her as you can. She's on to something about the power and the beauty of a woman. As long as a young lady carries herself with some type of class, it won't matter what stage she comes from, because men will see that and treat her with respect.

The conversation transitioned to a real sensitive subject. We asked about single mothers and bringing home men they are dating to meet their daughter.

You know it's an interesting call. I think a woman

should be sure that this guy has male qualities that should be exhibited around her daughter. Whatever person you bring around your young daughter, male or female, those are the people who are going to influence them.

If they are around them, the way they walk, talk, and handle things is what will influence them. I think that the mothers should date the guy a few months before bringing him around her daughter. People should send their representative after the first 30 days (laughter).

You send the best thing your mother raised in the first 30 days. After that, you start to see traces of who people are and of what they are really about. Because once you have been together 30 days, people start letting down their walls. I would think a woman should want to date a man 3 to 6 months before bringing him home. You don't want your daughters to have the perception that your home is a revolving door.

Given the number of terrible stories about young girls being taken advantage of, by men; we wondered what age Gary felt that a girl should be taught that the world can be very unforgiving.

As soon as she can talk (laughter), it's especially important for young ladies, because we live in a perception-based society. There are things that young ladies and women can't get away with that men can. No, it's not fair, but it just is the way it is.

It's a perception-based issue that from a young age girls are taught to be women. I mean they teach them how to be a mom real early on, like when they give a girl a baby doll. The baby doll spits-up, it boo-boos, it urinates; it does all that stuff, and girls learn how to work with that. So that's what they're taught from a very early age.

Boys are taught just the opposite. We're taught to be rough. We're given guns, toy soldiers and learn how to kill, destroy and defend. These are the messages that we're given from the beginning, so when you're dealing with young girls you have to start telling them as early as possible how to deal with a lot of barbaric young men.

Young men mature a whole lot later because of the things that are thrown at them early on. It's a lot of territorial things thrown at young men. A lot of fighting and things that go on with young men is because they always feel a need to prove themselves.

With young ladies, you should teach them as early as they can walk and talk. "Hey you should eat this way or hold your fork like this."

All of these are etiquette things and they should be taught as early as possible, because there are too many outside influences. I mean when these kids grow up, they may go to school with kids who aren't being taught some of these things, and kids are the best teachers for each other. We learn more from our peers then we do from our parents sometimes, so I think it's important to start enforcing these things as early as a kid can start to walk and talk especially if it's a young lady.

As we wrapped up the conversation, Gary offered his opinion on the matriculation of girls to womanhood to share with mothers.

I would simply say to know that we live in a society that evaluates things at a different rate and at a different level then you do. Young women will always mature faster. Know the difference between a man and a boy. Always keep your virtue and always keep your class about yourself. Women mature faster than men, so I would encourage young ladies to keep the focus on themselves. Mothers, put your girls before your relationships.

REFLECTION PERIOD

REFLECTION PERIOD

CURTAIN
CALL

"God, you have shown me so much favor that I don't even know where to start thanking you."

I have said that on more than one occasion with God in the conversations we have during my daily three-mile walk. I prefer walking alone while I am in 'Our" space because problems get worked out, thoughts flow more easily and those thoughts are clearer. Working on this project has been such a blessing to me both personally and professionally.

I have always been a writer. All of us have a special talent that we were gifted with, but until recently, my writing has been for only me, my family and friends, church and civic programs and a few articles here and there. For this work to be on this scale is amazing to and for me. I mean interviewing THESE men about THESE subjects; I have no words.

Having worked with kids for 20 years, I know how valuable this information is. The world has changed so much, and there are so many negative influences affecting OUR children. I feel that my participation in this is what I am supposed to do. I feel that this is how I am supposed to give back.

As a woman, I have learned so much from these gentlemen. I've always thought having been partly raised by my seven uncles would have given me more of an insight into men's psyche more than other women not fortunate enough to have had that experience.

My extended family is very close. My uncles would state that they were sharing 'this or that' with me so that I wouldn't be taken advantage of, or so that I would be a respectable young woman. Writing this reminded me of how loved I felt when they would talk to me about stuff. While I do still believe that their sharing gave me more of a heads up, there were certain responses to the asked questions that caused me to stop and think about what was said.

As I am maturing, I feel more and more that I am becoming one of "The Enlightened." The fact that God has blessed me with this opportunity is an experience for which I will eternally be grateful.

Oh, I would like to share one more thing. I love cooking and making gourmet foods. For me, conducting these interviews was like choosing six different spices to make the perfect dish. Combining the six of them made the perfect man.

Thank you for my opportunity.

Karen Watts M.Ed.

ENCORE

LISA WU HARTWELL FROM THE BRAVO HIT-SHOW REAL HOUSEWIVES OF ATLANTA WILL BE NATIONAL SPOKEPSERSON FOR "SAVING OUR DAUGHTERS" BOOK SERIES TO EMPOWER SINGLE PARENT MOTHERS

If you caught the last episode of RealHousewives of Atlanta Reunion, you can see that Lisa Wu Hartwell is not a woman you can just walk over and say something crazy too. Wow!! This is why It's Cool To Be Smart spoke with Lisa's publicist, Mr. "Carlos Scott of N-Vision Marketing Inc" on having her represent the Saving Our Daughters Book series as one of the national spokespersons, to help inspire mothers who have suffered from bad relationships in the past; but have overcame those circumstances. "Saving Our Daughters" books mirrors our organization efforts of empowering single parent mothers and daughters in the urban communities across the country" stated Curtis B. Executive Director of It's Cool To Be Smart".

On Friday December 19th, Lisa will kick off her commitment for single parent mothers by participating in the 4th Annual Bratz Toy Giveaway

"Affirm your daughter daily. Build up her confidence at home so the world will not be able to break her down".

LISA

for single parent mothers and their daughters from ages 6-9 at Princeton Elementary; right before Christmas. Other book celebrity participants will include, "Teen star Doc Shaw of "House of Payne", T.I., Rapper Bone Crusher, Tyler Perry Actor, Gary Sturgis and Sean Garrett.

Lisa will also be supporting the book by attending community platforms for single parent mothers and daughters on issues of domestic violence; teen pregnancy/HIV and Aids; and overcoming low esteem.

Lisa is a true role model for our single parent mothers and daughters in our communities. For more information on "Saving Our Daughters", please visit us at www.amanspointofview.org

---

ACTRESS KESHIA KNIGHT PULLIAM JOINS INFLUENTIAL WOMEN FOR 2ND ANNUAL *"SMART GIRLS WITH COOL JOBS"*

Young ladies at Towers High School were recently privileged to first-rate advice provided by business women from all over the nation. Hosted by It's Cool To Be Smart, Towers'female students listened to seven expert panelists who gave them advice on how to be successful in business, law, entertainment and journalism. The forum gave students the opportunity to receive words of wisdom from actress Keshia Knight Pulliam (House of Payne and new movie Tyler Perry's Madea Goes to Jail); Denise Hendricks, an Associate Producer of the Oprah Winfrey Show; Vikki Johnson, Public Affairs Manager for Black Entertainment Television (BET); entertainment lawyer and Governor on the Atlanta Chapter of the GRAMMY Awards Board Omara Harris; Monique Harris, the Executive Producer of Atlanta's CBS "Better Mornings Show;" and celebrity non-profit tax lawyer Shannon Nash. The women spoke to the girls about tackling low self-esteem, developing resumes that ref lect their talents, and standing strong in the face of peer pressure. "Be a person of integrity, be a person of your word. When you say you are going to do something—do it," Denise Hendricks said. "Be passionate about your goals and take initiative to fulfill them." She was encouraging the girls to begin preparing for their future careers by getting involved in extracurricular activities and pre-college internships.

"No matter your skill set or your interests; there is room for you," added Vikki Johnson.

"You are beautiful because you are you. Regardless of what other people look like or what clothes they are wearing, beauty is what is on the inside".

KESHIA

Page Designed by Trendsetters to Trendsetters Magazine

Contact Information | Personal Biography
Dr. Carman S. Clark

cclark4942@aol.com

Doctorate of Education, Counseling Psychology
University of Sarasota, Sarasota, Fl

Master of Arts, Clinical Psychology
Georgia School of Professional Psychology, Atlanta, Georgia

Public Health Education Studies
Emory University School of Public Health, Atlanta, Georgia

Bachelor of Arts, Psychology/Human Relations
Chapman University, Orange, California

Dr. Carman Suzanne Clark was born on January 31, 1964 in Alexandria, Louisiana, to a single parent household. She grew up not knowing her father. She has one sister on her father's side and three brothers on her mother's side. Presently, she is married, 24 years to Harold S. Clark, Jr. and they have two adult children, a daughter, Jennifer and a son, Alex. Their home of residence is in Atlanta, Georgia.

Dr. Clark is the author of two books with more pending. The first book, "Secrets of a Bayou Mystique," has been published by Christian Services Publishing, Inc. The book focuses on the devastating effects of child sexual abuse; offers suggestions for healing; discusses the need for establishing and nurturing a spiritual life; profiles and characterizes the sexual predator, the child abuser and their enablers; and stresses the omnipotent importance of holding on to the virtues of the spirit to get through the most difficult times of the healing process.

Her second book "Secrets Unfold" serves as a resource guide for family members, friends, co-workers, associates, etc. who would like to understand and know how to successfully help someone who has been sexually abused.

Her Educational background includes a Doctorate of Education in Counseling Psychology, Master of Arts in Clinical Psychology, Master's degree studies in Public Health Education, Bachelor of Arts in Psychology and Human Relations, and an Associate of Science in Medical Technology. She maintains multiple specialties in areas of medicine, psychology, education and forensics.

Professional Specialties include a private consulting practice in Clinical Psychology and Psychoanalysis, where she focuses on the treatment of conditions associated with post-traumatic stress disorders, psychological trauma, depression, anxiety, and issues of faith and spirituality; as well as life issues marked by painful and constricting patterns of behavior which are enduring, repetitive, and interfere with the appreciation of oneself and others. The objective is to help others better understand their inner private lives and developmental issues, from infancy to adulthood, which may have contributed to their present understanding of the environment.

With her specialty in Clinical Forensics, Dr. Clark did her dissertation research in the Department of Juvenile Justice, which demonstrated biological evidence of severe anxiety in children serving time in juvenile detention. Significant in the study was the revelation that the psychological needs of children in juvenile justice are not being adequately met. Dr. Clark is always available to consult on issues involving children in the juvenile justice system.

She also writes programs and conducts education seminars aimed at reducing domestic violence, child abuse, and substance abuse/addiction, with focused attention on the victim; as well as educating the public about HIV/AIDS, sexually transmitted diseases, and improving the personal quality of one's life.

Having been trained as a television show producer, her future goals include DVD and television show productions which will focus on issues of faith, spirituality and improving quality of life.

As an allied healthcare professional for over 25 years, Dr. Clark first received clinical medicine training in laboratory medicine at the United States Air Force's prestigious School of Healthcare Sciences at Sheppard Air Force Base in Whichita Falls, Tx.

From there she continued training at Malcolm Growe USAF Medical Center, which served the needs of military elites and distinguished politicians. She transferred to David Grant Medical Center at Travis AF Base in California, where she finished a distinguished military career of ten years in clinical medicine.

Her military service included deployment to Operation Desert Storm as a medical specialist in Blood Banking. Dr. Clark continues to serve as consultant, technical director and manager of a clinical laboratory program that she designed, developed, and built. The laboratory program maintains multiple medical specialties, including internal medicine, orthopedics, and cardiology; employs some 30 physicians, and serves over 250,000 patients a year.

The laboratory also acts as a reference lab for area hospitals and clinics. Her work history includes Emory University Hospital, Crawford Long Hospital at Emory University, Children's Healthcare of Atlanta, Peachtree Behavioral Medicine Hospital, Brawner Behavioral Health Systems, Walton County Medical Center, and Emergency Room Medicine.

Growing up deeply entangled within the bayou marshes of Louisiana's delta bayou, life began humble and simple, but Dr. Clark has remained tied to her roots, her people and her African-American heritage.

Facing the landscape of an open field, imagine an old, large wooden framed house, dull, gray, and withering as evidenced by dry peeling paint and three concrete steps removed from the front porch. This was her grandmother's house during early childhood, her favorite place. She knew her history as it was often handed down to her by word of mouth sometimes from her grandmother; or an elder uncle sitting in the dust on a coca-cola crate; or a faith-healer sharing words of faith and wisdom.

She was born in a space and time reeking with the bitter-sweet nostalgia of raw racism, Jim Crow laws and strong black family ties. Dr. Clark has also penned her own deeply troubling childhood life experiences in her first book; experiences that almost claimed her life three times.

Through it all, two things remained constant; her thirst for knowledge and her pursuit of wisdom. She is a shining example of the aphorism, "it's not where you live; it's how you live," and she has chosen to live with the purpose of helping others and sharing the virtues she learned to help make life more meaningful for everyone, one person at a time.

"The most important thing I've tried to instill in my daughter Chandler is the power she has. When the time comes for her to start dating and eventually get married, I want her to be able to choose someone who treats her well.

I don't want her to ever settle for less or feel that she has to. I make it a priority to continually build up her confidence and independence. She knows that counting on others to do for her is not an option. Having a man her life will be her option and never a necessity for her feelings of self-worth.

She will always know how a real man treats a woman and will accept nothing less. A young man is really going to have to bring his 'A' game to get next to my daughter because she's going to see right through him if he's not on point."

Russ Parr | Nationally Syndicated Host - Russ Parr Morning Show

REFLECTION PERIOD

REFLECTION PERIOD

REFLECTION PERIOD

REFLECTION PERIOD

Printed in the United States
145612LV00001B